CW00505687

POPE LEO XIII

Knights of Columbus

ILLUSTRATED

A complete ritual and history of the first three degrees, including all secret "work." By a former member of the order.

Profusely Illustrated

An Historical Sketch of the Institution

by

THOS. C. KNIGHT

1920

Ezra A. Cook

Publisher

26 E. Van Buren St., Chicago, Ill.

Table of Contents

"At the devil's booth are all things sold;
Each ounce of dross costs its ounce of gold.
For a cap and bells our lives we pay,
Bubbles we earn with a whole soul's tasking,
'Tis heaven alone that is given away;
'Tis only God may be had for the asking."

Lowell

PUBLISHER'S PREFACE

During the past years the many activities in which the Knights of Columbus have been engaged, both political and religious, have brought them before the public notice continually, thus creating a tremendous demand for literature concerning the Order.

For an organization that has been in existence so short a time to have reached a membership of nearly one half a million seems phenomenal, but such are the facts. It has been the rapid growth of the Fraternity which has prevented the Publishers from presenting the public with a complete ritual heretofore, as the ritual has been changed several times, and not until the order had adopted something like a permanent work did the Publishers feel warranted in issuing this publication. After having made careful investigations, and having had the present work authenticated, we feel great confidence in now placing this ritual before the public as complete, with signs, passwords and grips, giving in detail a full history and general sketch of the progress of the Society, with information which has heretofore been unpublished, concerning the objects and requirements of membership in this organization.

Being a religious, as well as a secret order, its secret workings have aroused unusual interest, and the Publishers feel that they have satisfied a general demand in presenting this volume, with the full First Three Degrees.

This exposition, while being issued complete, and as giving the authentic work now used in all Knights of Columbus Councils, is not issued with any malice towards the organization. It is not intended as an exposure, but is intended as a guide to those contemplating joining the Order, who desire previous information regarding the organization, and it is also intended that present members who are desirous of obtaining a higher degree may use this volume in attaining greater proficiency in the various degrees.

THE PUBLISHER.

CHRISTOPHER COLUMBUS

KNIGHTS OF COLUMBUS

An Historical Sketch

The Knights of Columbus is a Roman Catholic organization whose membership is confined to men affiliated with that church. Taking its name from the discoverer of America, it is interesting to note that the first Council to receive a charter was given the name of San Salvador, the island on which Columbus landed in 1492.

The moving spirit in promoting the birth of the order was the Reverend M. J. McGivney, then curate of Saint Mary's Church in New Haven, Connecticut. He was ably assisted by the Reverend P. P. Lawler, Cornelius T. Driscoll, Michael Curran, William M. Geary, Bartholomew Healey, Daniel Colwell, John T. Gorrigan, Dr. M. C. O'Conner, and James T. Mulligan.

13

Through their efforts an organization was effected at New Haven on February 2, 1882, and as incorporators, a charter secured under the laws of Connecticut, on March 29 of the same year. As defined by the charter the purposes of the society are:

1. To furnish insurance to its members, and at least temporary financial aid to the families of deceased members.

2. To develop practical Catholicity among its members.

3. To promote Catholic education and charity.

Such are the avowed purposes of the founders. In its organization, however, there was an unexpressed but clearly defined purpose which has no doubt immeasurably accelerated its growth. For ages there has been a lack of harmony between the Catholic clergy and Secret Societies in general.

The mysteries of an oath-bound, secret organization, meeting behind guarded doors, admission to which can be gained only by whispered words; a friendly grip of the hand that carries with it the thrill and remembrance of common experiences, and at the same time adds a feeling of ease and security even among strangers —these have been alluring to men in all times, but have never been favorably received by the Catholic clergy.

To combat the influences of such societies outside the pale of the church, the idea was evolved of supplying to the men a society combining all of the elements of a secret order, and at the same time keeping its movements under surveillance of the Catholic clergy, as may be witnessed by the following conditions of membership:

1. All Apostolic Delegates, Cardinals, Archbishops and Bishops are Ex-Officio members of the order, entitled to admittance on all occasions.

2. All Priests, secular and regular, may join the order without examination, but must pay their dues to remain in good standing.

3. All male members of the Catholic Church who are over sixteen years of age, and in good standing, are eligible. They must, however, show that they are Catholics, have made their last Easter duty, are willing and will pledge themselves to live up to the laws of the church.

Application for membership may be made by candidates fulfilling these requirements and their petitions ballotted upon at any regular meeting of a council. If elected the candidates may be initiated and admitted to full membership in the order. Initiations are given to classes of ten or more candidates. The larger the class the more lasting and impressive are the lessons taught through the ceremonies of the initiation.

In order to become a candidate for membership in this organization, the party desirous of joining must have a Knight in good standing present his name before a meeting; application blank will be furnished him, which must be signed by his Parish Priest; this is turned over

to the investigating committee, who pro-
ceeds in the usual way to find out what-
ever facts are obtainable concerning the
applicant's reputation, health, moral and
financial standing. If the investigating
committee reports favorably, the applicant is notified to attend for initiation.
An initial fee of $5.00 is usually required,
which is refunded in case of rejection. If
the applicant is accepted, the additional
fee, usually $10.00, is paid before his
initiation, but in some cases this can be
paid in installments within thirty or sixty
days.

The committees of the Knight of Columbus do not differ from those of other
secret societies, odd numbers being the
rule.

KNIGHTS OF COLUMBUS

Chronological and Statistical

Founded Feb. 2, 1882.
First Subordinate Council Established
　May 15, 1882.
First State Council Established 1892.
National Council Established 1893.
Number of State Councils, 1917,—52.
Number of Subordinate Councils, 1754.
Two Classes of Membership.
　Insurance Class.
　Associate Class.
Associate Class Admitted 1893.
Number in Insurance Class, 1914. 106,281
Number in Associate Class, 1914. 220,577
　Total Belonging 1914........326,858
　Total Belonging 1917........368,135
Insurance in Force 1914....$112,286,750
Death Claims paid during
　year ending June 30, 1914　　723,475
Death Claims paid to date..　7,308,682

Assessments Collected to
date 14,066,873
First Initiation in 4th Degree, Feb. 22,
1900.
Number in Class, First Initiation, 1,200.

The Knights of Columbus issues insurance policies in sums of one, two and three thousand dollars to members between the ages of 18 and 60 years, who are able to meet the requirements of a physical examination by a medical inspector. The rates of insurance are adjusted every five years, until a member has attained the age of 60, when a flat rate, based upon his age at initiation, becomes operative.

During the fiscal year ending June 30, 1914, death claims amounting to $723,475 were paid to beneficiaries. Since its organization death claims amounting to $7,308,682 have been paid by the society. On January 1, 1905, there were in force 43,537 policies, while on January 1, 1914, there were in force 106,281 policies, aggregating $112,286,750.

The organizers, on May 15, 1882, met at New Haven, Connecticut, in a body known as The Supreme Council, and instituted the first subordinate council, which they styled "San Salvador Council Number 1 of New Haven." Subordinate councils multiplied rapidly, but were confined to the limits of Connecticut until April 15, 1885, when one was instituted at Westerly, Rhode Island. At the present time the Order has subordinate councils firmly established in every state in the United States, in every province in the Dominion of Canada, in Cuba, Porto Rico, Newfoundland, the Philippine Islands and Alaska.

Owing to the rapid growth of the Order, one of the difficult problems has been that of regulating the number of members entitled to seats in the Supreme Council. The first effort resulted in a law declaring that this body should thereafter consist of the Supreme Committee and one delegate for each fifty members of the several subordinate councils. Under this apportionment the Supreme Council soon became so unwieldly that on May 14, 1886, the Supreme Council, by resolution, became a Board of Government composed of the former Supreme Committee as Directors, and giving to the Grand Knight and Past Grand Knight of each subordinate council a voice and vote in its deliberations. As the Order extended its activities into the various states, the Board of Government again found it necessary to decrease the number of delegates. This was done by considering the Board of Government as the National body and providing for State Councils, composed of two delegates from each subordinate council in the state. The name "Board of Government" was dropped and that of National Council adopted. The National Council consists of the State Deputy of each State Council and one delegate from every 1,000 members of the insurance class.

The creation of the National Council was followed in October, 1893, by the recognition of an entirely new and distinct class of members known as Associate Members. This class admits to membership men of advanced years, and those who, because of physical disability, are unable to pass the physical examination; and, finally, all men of Catholic allegiance not desiring the insurance features.

It is probably due to this latter class, numbering, on January 1, 1914, 220,577 members, as against 106,281 members in the insurance class, that has caused the Order to develop the social, educational, and charitable work in a marked degree. Notable work has been performed by the Order in promoting Catholic education, providing homes for Catholic orphans, endowing scholarships in C a t h o l i c colleges, providing lectures on Catholic doctrine, maintaining employment bureaus, and performing works of similar character. On every battle-field of Europe and in every cantonment of our own country, the Knights are found ministering to the wounded, the sick and disconsolate, while adding words of cheer and encouragement to the more fortunate. In 1904 the Catholic University at Washington was given the sum of $50,000 for the endowment of a Chair of American

History. "Columbus Day," the observation of which has been legalized by the legislatures of fifteen states, is due mainly to the influence of the Knights of Columbus. These states are California, Colorado, Connecticut, Illinois, Kentucky, Maryland, Massachusetts, Michigan, Missouri, Montana, New Jersey, New York, Ohio, Pennsylvania and Rhode Island.

Being national in character, the society has been largely instrumental in securing by the United States Government the splendid monument in Washington, erected to the memory of Columbus. As he gave to the world a new continent, it is but mete that the Knights should endeavor to bring that continent under the influence of religion, good-will to men, and loyalty to the nation.

A Fourth Degree was added to the work of the Knights of Columbus on February 22, 1900, when a class of 1,200 candidates was initiated in New York City. These came from every section of the United States. The requirement for membership in this degree is that a candidate has been a member of the Third Degree for a period of two years just passed.

In 1908 there appeared a new Order under the name of The Order of the Alhambra, and claiming to be a higher and more select branch of the Knights of Columbus. Its candidates are chosen from the members of the Third and Fourth degrees. This Order has been bitterly opposed by the Hierarchy of the Church on the grounds that its ceremonies are entirely foreign to the work of the Knights of Columbus.

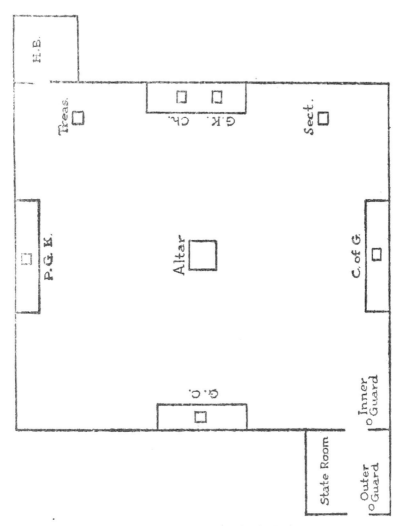

DIAGRAM OF LODGE ROOM
(FIRST DEGREE)

CHAPTER I.

GRAND KNIGHT.
CHAPLAIN.
PAST GRAND KNIGHT.
GRAND CHANCELLOR.
CAPTAIN OF THE GUARD.
SECRETARY.
TREASURER.
INNER GUARD.
OUTER GUARD.

Officers are elected by secret ballot, holding office for one year, with the exception of the Chaplain and Outer and Inner Guards. The Chaplain is usually the Parish Priest. The Outer and Inner Guards are appointed by the Grand Knight.

CHAPTER II.

INSTRUCTION

OPENING.

Your council should be opened promptly at the hour named in the By-Laws, and its business conducted without unnecessary delay. Nothing so deters members from constant attendance as long, tiresome sessions.

LAWS.

The lawsof the Order and your own By-Laws should often be discussed. Your most valuable members are those who have an understanding of the laws.

RITUAL

Your officers should commit the charges to memory; this will add more to the fame and honor of your council than anything else.

SECRET WORK.

The secret work should be practiced as often as circumstances will permit. It

28

will give your officers confidence in themselves, and teach your members the mode and use of the secret signs and words.

REGALIA.

The regalia shall be kept in the anteroom. Members will decorate themselves there, and thereby avoid confusion and forgetfulness.

VISITORS.

Visitors, when unknown, must be thoroughly examined by the Captain of the Guard before admission. Every courtesy should be extended to visitors; it will greatly improve the reputation of your council.

SOCIAL.

Visits, as a council to other councils, are greatly to be recommended; the latent blessings and virtues of our Order will, through such means, be brought into active play.

RITUALISTIC LAWS.

The forms and language of the Ritual are law, and innovations or departure from them are positive and direct violation of the Order.

LODGE CONDUCT.

The affairs of your council should be conducted on strict business and social principles. Your business should be governed by nothing but the laws governing the Order; your social intercourse by the strict etiquette of good society.

SUPERIORS.

In true accordance with military and fraternal usage, Superiors are to be looked up to as guides, and to be obeyed in all things pertaining to the discipline and welfare of the Order.

CHAPTER III.

ORDER OF BUSINESS

1. The Secretary will read the minutes of the last regular meeting.

   Approval and corrections according to regular parilamentary law.

2. READING OF APPLICATIONS FOR MEMBERSHIP.

   The Grand Knight will investigate the applications and appoint the investigating committee.

3. REPORTS OF INVESTIGATING COMMITTEES.

   Unfavorable reports dispense with the need of balloting. A favorable ballot elects to membership.

4. BALLOTING FOR APPLICANTS.

   White balls elect; one black ball rejects. Errors may be corrected by re-balloting.

5. READING OF COMMUNICATIONS.

Communications will be read by the Secretary, and filed or acted upon at the discretion of the Grand Knight or by motion of the Council.

6. READING OF BILLS.

The Finance Committee will pass on all bills before they are submitted to the Council by the Treasurer.

7. REPORT OF STANDING COMMITTEES.

8. REPORT OF SPECIAL COMMITTEES.

9. UNFINISHED BUSINESS.

Initiations—ceremonies are carried out.

10. NEW BUSINESS AND SECRET WORK.

11. RECESS.

Dues may be paid at this time.

12. GOOD OF THE ORDER.

13. REPORT OF SECRETARY.

14. REPORT OF THE TREASURER.

15. CLOSING CEREMONY.

CHAPTER IV.

OPENING CEREMONIES.

(The Grand Knight will go to his chair and call the Council to order by one rap with the gavel.)

Grand Knight—I am about to open... ..... Council No.... of the Knights of Columbus. All persons not qualified to remain will now retire.

When the Council Chamber is free from intrusion, the Captain of the Guard will distribute *the ribbons to the* officers, who will pin them on their lapels.

Grand Knight (one rap)—.....Council .... will now come to order. Brothers, remember your obligations. The Captain of the Guard will take the pass word.

The Outer and Inner Guards take their places; the officers take their chairs; the Captain of the Guard takes the password. Both passwords are taken up in the

Chamber, outer and inner. Any ordinary lodge room may be used as a Council Chamber.

The Grand Knight will occupy the highest chair. At his right the Chaplain, when present, will take his place.

The official chair on the right side of the Chamber will be held by the Past Grand Knight. The official chair opposite the high chair will be filled by the Grand Counsellor.

The official chair on the left side of the Chamber will be filled by the Captain of the Guard.

The Secretary and Treasurer will have their places on either side of the Grand Knight.

One rap calls the Council to order; two raps call the officers to their feet; three raps call the Council to its feet.

Grand Knight—Brother Secretary, call the roll of officers.

The officers stand and answer present as called by the Secretary, in the order of their seniority.

OFFICERS IN ORDER OF SENIORITY

Grand Knight................Present

Chaplain ....   "

Past Grand Knight...........   "

Grand Counsellor.............   "

Captain of the Guard.........   "

Secretary ....   "

Treasurer ....   "

Inner Guard..................   "

Outer Guard..................   "

Grand Knight (three raps)—Knights, Brothers: We are now engaged in the noble work of our Order. Remember your promises and prove yourselves true Knights, loyal sons of the Holy Mother Church. We will now sing the opening ode.

Air: "COLUMBIA"

Columbian Knights here united,
    Let each one his pledges renew;
By valor great wrongs may be righted
    And aid brought the honest and true.
Our patriotic precepts require us
    To love and protect this free land;
Let fraternity ever inspire us
    To deeds that are noble and grand.

Chaplain invokes the blessing (if he be present; if absent, the invocation may be omitted).

"May the blessing of Almighty God, Father, Son and Holy Ghost, descend upon us and remain with us forever. Amen."

The regular order of business is now carried out, as shown in the previous chapter.

CHAPTER V.

CLOSING CEREMONIES.

Grand Knight—Knights, Brothers: I am about to close.......... Council No. ...., Knights of Columbus. Let your light shine before the world, that the world may see the beauty of the Holy Mother Church and be led to the unity of true Christian brotherhood. We will sing the closing ode:

CLOSING ODE.

Air: "AULD LANG SYNE"

Now on life's voyage we set forth,
　　An earnest faithful crew;
We journey east, west, south and north,
　　For the good that we can do.

And be the voyage long or short,
　　And though the waves roll high,
We will safely reach the further port,
　　On our bark we can rely.

Then on life's voyage we will set forth,
　　An earnest, faithful crew,
We will journey east, west, south and north,
　　For the good that we can do.

39

CHAPTER VI.

THE FIRST DEGREE.

Initiations are conducted in classes of ten or more.

The candidates are assembled in the ante-room.

All candidates must have signed an application giving their names, ages, occupation, parish, and present a signed statement of their priest that they have made their Easter duty or have been to the sacraments at least once a year.

These certificates dispense with all examination in the ante-room.

The first degree is to test the faith of the candidates and to teach them the responsibility of the act of faith.

In all the degrees, the essential idea alone is to be safeguarded. The officers in charge are left to their own wisdom and ingenuity in coining words that will impress the candidates.

Unlike all other Orders, there is no inviolate verbal form of ritual. This wise method prevents a mechanical, parrot-like committing to memory of words and phrases, and allows the officers to develop their originality to the utmost.

COUNCIL CHAMBER.

Grand Knight—Captain of the Guard, you will take your guards to the ante-room and lead in the candidates.

The Captain and as many guards as are necessary, go to the ante-room and line up the candidates. The lights in the Council Chamber are dimmed.

Then, to the sound of the organ, the candidates file into the chamber and are led around the room. The Council may sing some march tune, such as "Come, Holy Ghost."

COME, HOLY GHOST, CREATOR BLEST.

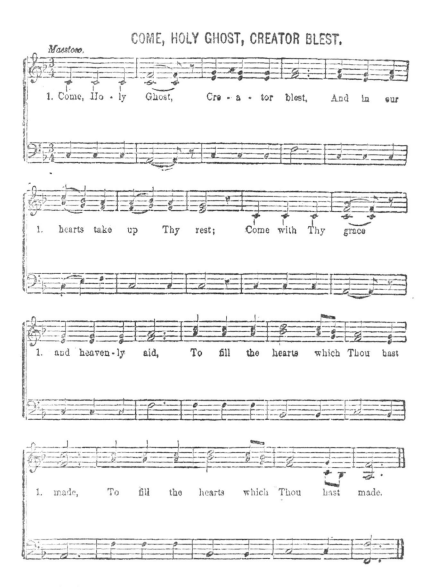

Maestoso.

1. Come, Ho - ly Ghost, Cre - a - tor blest, And in our

1. hearts take up Thy rest; Come with Thy grace

1. and heaven - ly aid, To fill the hearts which Thou hast

1. made, To fill the hearts which Thou hast made.

When all have been lined about the room, one light is allowed to burn dimly before the center altar, the Grand Knight will advance to the center and say:

44

Grand Knight—Gentlemen, before you may go further into the Order of the Knights of Columbus, it is necessary for you to make an act of faith. Let every one answer for himself.

Q. Do you believe in God?

A. I do.

Q. Do you believe in the three divine persons?

A. I do.

Q. Do you believe in the Holy Roman Catholic Church?

A. I do.

Q. Do you pledge yourself to obey the Church in all that relates to faith and morals?

A. I do.

Q. Do you pledge yourself to be a true Knight of this Order and to obey its laws at all times?

A. I do.

Grand Knight—It is well. Remember that you are Catholics, and for the future you will be Catholic Knights, always prepared to defend your faith and to give to those who walk in darkness a reason for the faith that is in you.

Retire now to prepare for the second degree.

The organ plays a march. The Captain of the Guard and his men lead the candidates to the ante-room.

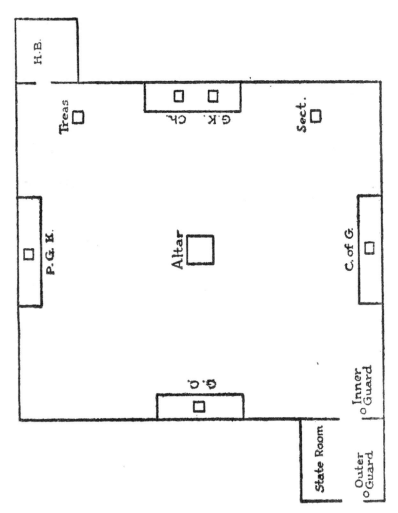

DIAGRAM OF LODGE ROOM
(SECOND DEGREE)

CHAPTER VII.

THE SECOND DEGREE.

The Captain of the Guard and his men go to the ante-room and prepare the candidates in line. At a given signal they march into the Council Chamber to the sound of the organ. They are not blindfolded, but the Chamber is dark except for one light over the center altar.

They march about the Chamber and form a hollow square, facing the center.

The Grand Knight and the other officers are before the center altar. The Captain of the Guard advances to them and salutes.

The Grand Knight, or some one appointed, may ask the questions of the candidates.

The lesson to be conveyed to them in the Second Degree is that most of them have no intelligent idea of what their faith consists of. They do not know even the catechism.

The contrast between their prompt avowal of their faith a few moments before in the First Degree, and the public exposure of their ignorance must be made as strong as possible by the officers of the Council.

The candidates must be impressed and stimulated to action, so that they may in the future spend more time in studying their religion and learning its tenets.

If they are ignorant, how can they expect to influence others and lead them into the Church?

Grand Knight—Brothers, you have affirmed your faith. You believe in Holy Mother Church. Are you able to defend her if necessary?

Thereupon, candidates are called by name and asked to repeat answers taken from the catechism. If there are any priests among the candidates, care must be taken to avoid asking them any questions.

The questioner is allowed great latitude in his questions. Much of the success of the degree depends upon the subtleness and ingenuity of the questioner. For example, the questioner calls upon Brother

.... :

Q. Brother ...., what is grace?

Q. How many kinds of grace are there?, etc.

After this catechetical quiz has gone on for some time, the Grand Knight gives the charge:

Grand Knight—Brothers: You have sworn to defend the faith. Yet you have immediately demonstrated that you are unable to do so.

You have failed in simple questions of the catechism. In former days, the clergy alone could instruct and guide the people; but today, the laity must be militant educators and light-bearers. The laity must assist the clergy. They must know their holy religion almost as well as the clergy.

You, Brothers, have had an example. Go from here, resolved that you will study your faith and be able to speak the word of truth upon the proper occasion.

Guards, lead the candidates to the ante-room to prepare for the Third Degree.

The candidates file out under the leadership of the guard.

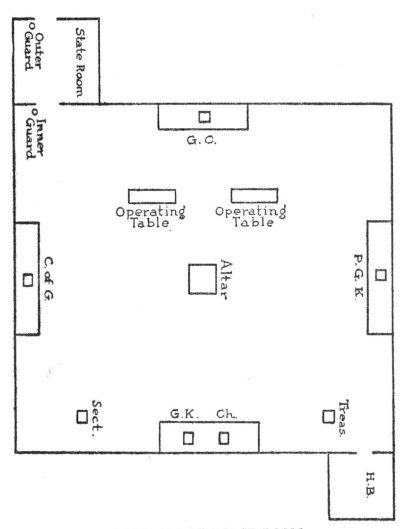

DIAGRAM OF LODGE ROOM

(THIRD DEGREE)

CHAPTER VIII.

THIRD DEGREE—PREPARATION.

THE TEAM.

The personnel of the team which gives this degree is as follows:

A Captain of the Guard in command of the team.

A Decoy Priest. He wears the ordinary street dress of the priest, with Roman collar and rabbi.

A Secret Service man incognito.

Enough initiated members to scatter through the candidates and urge them to action.

HOW ROBED.

Several robed assistants. The robe is made of any black cloth, fitted with a peaked cowl like a monk's habit.

Several doctors attired as for the operating room.

55

All members will wear black robes, entirely covering their regular habit, and will be masked.

The Grand Knight will appear as usual his ribbon of office his only adornment.

In the center of the Council Chamber will be a table with surgical instruments and bandages.

A small room leading from the Chamber will be made as warm as possible. This room is known as the Hot Box or the H. B.

When all is in readiness, the Grand Knight will direct the Captain of the Guard to send his men to their work.

The assistants go to the ante-room, where the candidates are gathered.

Their work is to stir up the candidates to anger if possible, using the decoy priest as a last recourse.

CHAPTER IX.

Line up the candidates in such a surly manner that they will take offense and refuse to go into line.

The line-up may be made according to seniority or in any fashion the team may judge efficient.

Often an old priest, if any priests are to be initiated, may be called to head the line. The assistants may try to confuse and anger him by mispronouncing his name or calling attention to his position. Generally, it is not wise to push the priest too-far. Laymen are better subjects, and the dignity of the priesthood must be preserved.

The best method to obtain results is to treat the candidates as though they were a crowd of school-boys, who needed a severe censure for every move made. If a candidate does not obey any order given to him, such as to stand for a certain position behind his fellow in line, to look straight ahead, etc., it is good to send him to the rear and hint that he may not be allowed to go on.

Break the spirit of all, if possible, and make all obey timidly the smallest command of the team members.

If the candidates rebel and refuse to go on, the Captain of the Guard will be called. He will enter, wearing any seemingly disreputable robe, such as a bath robe, which has been soaked in whiskey, and giving the candidates the impression that he is drunk. The decoy members will artfully stimulate this suggestion.

The Captain of the Guard will brutally inquire the cause of the trouble and when he has listened to the charges of the candidates and the answers of his assistants, he will deliver his judgment.

This is left to his ingenuity and histrionic skill. He will invite the candidates to remember that they came as gentlemen to join an Order of gentlemen, and that unless they show the manners of gentlemen, they will all be disbarred from further entrance into the Order. The candidates must trust the honor of the Order, and its greatness, and bear with any seemingly strange methods which they cannot understand at this time.

As a last recourse to stir up the candidates, the decoy priest will leave the line and walk away.

The Captain of the Guard will angrily question him:

"Why are you leaving your place?"

D. P. "I am sick. I want a glass of water."

C. G. "Go back to your place. No one may leave his place for any consideration."

D. P. "But I am sick and I must have a glass of water or I shall faint."

C. G. "Faint then."

He orders his assistants to take the decoy priest back by force if necessary.

Meanwhile, the Secret Service man slips away and comes back with a glass of water, which he hands to the decoy priest. As the decoy priest takes it, the Captain of the Guards leaps forward, angrily, and knocks the glass from his hand.

If the candidates have not yet gone beyond control, this always stirs them to fury, and they break ranks in angry confusion, struggling and shouting against the insult to the priest.

The decoy members of the team skillfully urge the stronger-willed candidates to shout defiance against the Captain of the Guard and his assistants.

They suggest that he is drunk and that it is an outrage—it is an insult to the priesthood.

Many refuse to go on, and threaten to break down the door and leave for good, if they are not released. Some try to catch the Captain of the Guard, but are skillfully kept away by the decoys.

The candidates are to be aroused to the last extreme of fury, but are to be handled so that they cannot do anything.

If the candidates are strong enough to overcome the guards and demand apologies and explanations, the Captain of the Guard is slipped away, and the Grand Knight comes out and quiets the tempest.

He will see that the man is punished if he is guilty. If they will be patient and allow the work to go on, the case will be taken care of in due time.

Then he goes back into the Council Chamber. The decoy priest helps to calm the candidates, by excusing the Captain of the Guard on account of his condition. He is not so much to be blamed because he is drunk. Gradually the candidates are calmed and go back into line.

CHAPTER X.

___

___

They are all blindfolded. They put their hands on shoulders. The guards give the signal, the doors are opened, and the candidates march into the Council Chamber. The organ is playing. They are marched around the room several times and halted in a hollow square facing the center. The blinds are removed. The doctors are seated around the table covered with surgical instruments and writing paper. The Grand Knight sits near the table.

The members of the Order, all covered with black robes, stand behind the candidates.

The chief surgeon stands up and calls several of the candidates and decoys. The guards lead them to the table.

Chief Surgeon—Before you may go further, you must show that you are worthy. You must submit to a test of your strength that will satisfy the Order that you are in earnest.

He calls on one of the decoys to take the first test.

Chief Surgeon—I have here a copy of the pledge which you must take to this Order. I have also a dagger (picking up from the table a dagger). You will take this dagger, bare your arm, prick your veins and sign this pledge with your own blood. Are you willing to take the test?

Decoy feigns reluctance, and plays that he is afraid to take the test.

Chief Surgeon—You must take the test or you cannot go on. Are you afraid of a little blood? There are doctors here who will see that you do not injure yourself. Do you call yourself a man—afraid of pricking a little vein?

Decoy—I cannot take such a pledge; you have no right to ask it.

Chief Surgeon—You will step aside for a moment. We shall take up your case at once. (Calls one of the candidates.)

Are you willing to take this dagger, prick a vein of your arm and sign your name to this pledge?

Generally the candidate says yes, and prepares to undertake the task. But, before he can do so, one of the guards whispers to the chief surgeon, who turns and addresses the candidates:

Chief Surgeon—While we are trying the case of this candidate, who has refused the pledge, it will be necessary for all of you to retire. The guards will lead you to the room, where you will remain until you are again summoned.

CHAPTER XI.

The organ plays, and the guards lead the candidates to the Hot Box. When they are all in, the door is fastened, and masked guards are stationed inside and outside of the door.

The Hot Box must be small enough to make it difficult to move about easily without jostling. The Captain of the Guard is found inside and mingles with the candidates. He is as surly as he was in the ante-room, and the candidates feel their anger rising against him.

The decoy priest soon complains of the heat and asks to be let outside. The Captain of the Guard refuses to let him go. They quarrel, and the decoy priest says he is going to go out whether the Captain of the Guard likes it or not.

The guards and decoys keep between the decoy priest, the Captain and the candidates. As the decoy priest starts to push the Captain aside, the Captain slaps him over the mouth.

The decoy priest reels from the blow, and blood seems to flow from his mouth. He has had some red gum in his mouth, which gives his sputum the appearance of blood.

At once there is an uproar. Some of the decoys shout to be let out, others pound upon the door, and the candidates are roused to fury, and try to reach the Captain of the Guard. The inside and outside guards and decoys must protect him and see that the door is opened before it is broken down.

Then all rush out into the Council Chamber, shouting and gesticulating. They rush to the table, where the Grand Knight and the doctors are sitting.

The Grand Knight and the doctors, assisted by the guards, try to make themselves heard. At last they succeed in quieting the confusion to such an extent that they can listen to the candidates, who desire to mount a chair and say what they wish.

CHAPTER XII.

―――

―――

If necessary, a decoy starts the part. He stands on a chair and bitterly denounces the whole procedure. They came as gentlemen, as Catholics, to enter an Order that has been approved by the Church, and they are subjected to the indignities of drunken brutes. Even the sacred character of the priest himself is not respected. God's holy anointed is brutally insulted and even struck by a drunken wretch.

He demands that the Captain of the Guard be summarily punished and thrown out of the meeting and the Order, and that the real work of the Order be taken up.

As many as wish may make speeches. The most hotheaded and devout generally make the best talks. Some of the priests make especially eloquent pleas against the whole procedure, and many of the laymen are discovered to be eloquent pleaders, who never before had dared to speak in public.

When all have finished, the Grand Knight stands upon the chair and begs them to be patient. He deprecates the unfortunate occurrence. The man will be tried at once. Seven men will be picked from their number as a jury. The charges will be made in due order, and the verdict of the jury will be received as final. Are they willing to abide by such a procedure?

They answer yes.

The candidates are then told to sit down in the chairs around the wall and the jury is selected.

The secret service man is one of the jurors.

The seven are called to the middle of the chamber and lined up before the table.

Grand Knight—Gentlemen, you must give up all your valuables, and have your pockets entirely empty so that you may hand nothing to one another during the trial.

I must ask the Captain of the Guard to go among you and receive all that you have on your person.

The Captain, amidst wild glares and murmurs, begins to take the things that the jurors hand over to him. Some generally are very angry at him and show it by their manner; some do not care to hand him anything.

The secret service man, especially, shows resentment, and at first refuses to give up anything. He objects to the procedure. One of the guards comes up to him and runs his hands over his clothes. He resists, and the guard calls out that he has a revolver in his pocket.

The Grand Knight asks him if it is true that he has a concealed weapon. He says that it is true. He is a secret service man and always carries a revolver.

The Grand Knight—You must give it up.

Secret Service Man—I will not give it up. I am under orders to carry it and never to allow it to pass from my possession.

The Grand Knight—Captain of the Guard, you will see that this gentleman gives up his weapon.

The Captain steps up to the secret service man and asks him for the weapon.

Secret Service Man—You dirty brute, I would not give it to you in any case.

The Captain catches hold of him and

tries to drag the gun from his pocket. They struggle, and the guards close around them.

Suddenly the revolver comes out in the secret service man's hand. Captain catches the hand and pulls it down, and then there is a flash and the sharp report of the weapon. The Captain reels backward, and blood pours out over his chest. He falls into the arms of the guards.

The Captain of the Guard has a rubber bag full of red fluid under his robe. This is pierced by a knife just before the shot, and gives the delusion of blood flowing from his breast.

Confusion reigns in the chamber. The priests rush to give the man absolution, some of the guards hurry away the secret service man, and the wounded Captain is carried out into the ante-room and the crowd is closed in the chamber.

Experience has shown that the body of the candidates is always in a strange condition of mind during this period of waiting. The members go about and whisper of the terrible accident, and hint of the scandal if the newspapers find out about the affair. If the secret service man dies, it will be the end of the Knights of Columbus.

The dramatic climax is worked up naturally until all the candidates are consumed with anxiety to know the worst.

After ten or fifteen minutes the door of the ante-room is opened, and the Grand

Knight walks into the chamber, followed by the doctors, the secret service man, and a well-dressed, clean looking man, whom all recognize as the Captain of the Guard, and the decoy priest.

The Grand Knight takes the middle of the floor, with the others around him, and begins to speak:

Grand Knight—Gentlemen and Brothers: When I have given the solution of the strange adventures which you have gone through this day, you will learn the most telling lesson ever devised to teach you that things are not always what they seem.

He turns to the decoy priest, and pulls off his collar and rabbi, saying:

Grand Knight—Our good friend and brother here is not a priest at all. He bore all the outward marks, but the inner seal of the sacrament of Orders has never been imprinted upon his soul. He was playing a part, and that he played it well, I know. For I can see upon the faces of all of you, the expression of relief which

81

comes to those who awake from a terrible dream and find that it was only a dream.

And this good brother (turning to the secret service man and taking him by the hand) is not a desperate criminal, with the blood of his fellow upon his head. Our old friend, the Captain of the Guard, stands here beaming upon us. A short time past, you wished almost to tear him to pieces. You thought him a brute; you believed him a sacrilegious wretch who dared to raise his hand against the Lord's anointed. It was a delusion. The good Captain and the good pseudo-father had conspired together to deceive you. See how they love each other! (The two shake hands heartily.)

Brothers, take this lesson to heart, and bear it with you in all your activities of life. Judge not by appearances. Things may not be what they seem. Suspend your judgment until there can be no mistake. Then act. Remember this lesson. Cherish it in your hearts.

You have seen that men are led. Under certain conditions men will do things that they never would do if they were alone or stopped to realize what their acts may lead to.

We asked you to take this dagger and let your own blood and write with your own blood your acceptance of our Order. We had no right to ask you to do such a thing. If you had insisted upon taking the pledge, you would have discovered that this dagger is a trick also. You could not have hurt yourselves. It is filled with red fluid, and when you pushed it against your arm, the red fluid would have flowed out and looked like blood (demonstrates with dagger). But it would have been wrong in intention anyway. If it had been a real dagger, some zealous brother would be sure to cut himself badly.

Learn the lesson of your rights as an individual. You are responsible before your conscience to God alone. No one has any right to ask you to do an act which is evil, no matter for what purpose. Remember this lesson.

A more important lesson has been put in dramatic form for you on this occasion. You were many. The guards were few. Yet they were able to control you from the ante-room to the climax you have just witnessed. Why? They were an organized unit and knew what they were doing. You were unorganized and did not know what to do. If at any moment, one or two of you had taken the lead and had gathered the forces of your body about you, you would have controlled and beaten the guards. Without leaders you were simply a mob, expending a great deal of energy, but accomplishing nothing.

Extend this lesson to your daily life. Study and work to be leaders of men. The world is sick because there are not enough in the active life of today who can visualize the meaning of life for mankind. As Knights of Columbus, you must be leaders. You are sons of the old Mother Church, who is the divinely appointed mother of men.

Study her; learn her ideals, her God-given means of saving the world, and as laymen be missionaries in every walk of life. We must assist our clergy in their laborious work of saving souls. They are our spiritual guides and leaders. We must become leaders of the world, under their direction, and bring to this sad earth the kingdom of God and the brotherhood of man. All must be united in one grand, glorious band of humanity under the one mother church.

"Remember, brothers, that the Church alone has the truth of God. We are her children. We must spread the truth. We have been given this blessing. As Knights of Columbus, we shall learn how to bring it to the whole world.

"This is my charge: Think on these things; cherish the memory of this hour.

"Raise your right hands and repeat after me this pledge of fealty to the Order:

" 'I now solemnly pledge myself to keep sacred the secrets of this Order; to be a loyal and true son of the Church, and a faithful member of the Knights of Columbus. I will always be ruled by knightly courtesy in my relations with my fellow men. I pledge myself to God, to His Holy Church, to my country, to mankind, to be always a true Knight. Amen.'

"It is well, brothers. I shall now declare this Council adjourned." (Either for recess or until the next regular meeting, according to the arrangement agreed upon beforehand.) "The older members will greet their new brothers and extend to them the courtesy of.......Council."

(Raps once.)

87

CHAPTER XIII.

THE SECRET WORK.

The secret work is made a part of the regular council meeting for the benefit of new members, usually at the first meeting following the initiation.

It is generally demonstrated by the Grand Knight, under the head of New Business.

The new members are led by the Captain of the Guard to the Grand Knight's chair.

The Grand Knight addresses them:

"Brothers, as duly accredited members of the Knights of Columbus, it is your right and your duty to become acquainted with the secret work of the Order.

"The password is important. It admits you to the Council Chamber. It must be kept a secret from all outsiders.

"The word is changed once a year. For the present year it is: (One password was 'Knights of Columbus shall rule.')

"When you come to a council meeting, attract the attention of the Outside Guard. Whisper in his ear the first half of the password. He will admit you into the ante-room. Rap upon the entrance of the Council Chamber. The Inside Guard will open the wicket and you will whisper into his ear the last half of the password. He will then admit you to the Council Chamber. You will walk to the center of the chamber and salute the Captain of the Guard with the usual military salute. When he returns the salute, you may take your place among the members of the council.

"The Grip: The grip is given by shaking hands in the ordinary way, and giv-

ing two distinct pressures with all the fingers. This is answered by one sharp pressure. The question which goes with the grip is, 'What council do you belong to?'

"If any brother is in distress or needs aid to accomplish any work, generally in a crowd, he will call out, 'Are there any good men here?' If there are any Knights of Columbus present, they will answer, 'Yes!' and come to his assistance.

"The training in the Third Degree will make it easy for a few to accomplish wonders even in a large crowd.

"Brothers, you are now duly accredited members of the Knights of Columbus. You are initiated into the secrets of the Order. You may come in and go out as children of one family. I charge you to be faithful to the Order; true to your pledge. Never reveal our secrets to outsiders.

"As Catholics you have all the sanctions of the Church to keep you faithful. We have the approval and blessing of the

Church. The Pope himself, our Most Holy Father, has given us his Apostolic benediction. If then—which may God forbid!—anyone is tempted to reveal our secrets, let him think well before he acts. Such a one would surely incur the curse of God. His name would become a by-word and a reproach among all honorable men. He would be shunned and cursed by all his former fellows, the conscience of a guilty wretch who has sold his soul, would sooner or later come home to him, to chastise him day and night until he made his peace with God and did true penance for his crime.

"It is impossible to imagine a brother who could be guilty of such an act. He must first become a renegade and an un-believer, and join himself to the forces of the devil, who prowls about the world seeking whom he may devour.

"He deserves the reception which the devil himself received from God—to be cast into eternal torture. Only the Infi-nite Mercy of God can save him from such a fate. Think well, then, brothers,

of your acts and be ever true Knights,
ready to do and die, if necessary, for the
honor of God and the glory of His Holy
Church. Amen."

SECRET SOCIETY RITUALS

Free Masonry

EXPLANATION.

The first three degrees, as published in "Ronayne's Hand Book," termed the Blue Lodge Degrees, are common to all the Rites. The Scotch Rite exclusively covers 30 Degrees (4th to 33d inclusive). Blue Lodge and Chapter, 7 Deg., or "Free Masonry Illustrated" 7 Degrees and "Knight Templarism Illustrated" 6 Degrees include the entire "York Rite' 'or "American Rite" Degrees. The York and Scotch rites are the leading Masonic Rites.

HAND BOOK OF FREE MASONRY;

By Edmond Ronayne, Past Master of Keystone Lodge, No. 639, Chicago. Latest Revised Edition, with portraits enlarged to 284 pages, 85 illustrations.

Paper cover, pocket size....................$ .75
Flexible cloth   "   "   gilt top.... 1.25

This work gives the correct or "Standard" work and ritual of Masonry; the proper position of each officer in the Lodge room, order of opening and closing the Lodge, dress of candidate, ceremony of initiation, the correct method of conferring the three degrees of "Ancient Craft Masonry," Entered Apprentice, Fellow Craft and Master Mason, the proper manner of conducting the business of the Lodge, and giving the signs, grips, pass-words, etc., all of which are

Accurately Illustrated With 85 Engravings.

The oaths, obligations and lectures are quoted verbatim and can be relied upon as correct. In short, it is a complete and accurate Lodge manual. The high standing of Mr. Ronayne in the fraternity; his popularity and success as a teacher and lecturer in the lodge, together with testimony of high Masonic authority, leaves no doubt of the accuracy of this work. It contains the written and the "unwritten" work. No higher proof of the accuracy and reliability of this ritual could be given, than that it is

Used Extensively in the Lodges by Officials
as a guide to the ceremonies, members of the fraternity use it to refresh their memories on the lectures and ceremonies, in short it is the "Blue Lodge Complete." Sent securely wrapped on receipt of price.

BLUE LODGE AND CHAPTER.

By Edmond Ronayne. Bound in fine Cloth, 604 pages.

Price $2.00

This book comprises the Hand Book of Free Masonry, which gives the written and the "unwritten" work of the three degrees of Blue Lodge Masonry, and the complete work of the four degrees of Chapter Masonry, including the Royal Arch degree. This makes a compact, handy and economical volume.

REVISED ILLINOIS FREEMASONRY, ILL'D.

The complete and accurate ritual of the First Seven Masonic Degrees of the Blue Lodge and Chapter, by a Past High Priest, with all Monitorial and Scripture Readings and the Secret Work fully illustrated. The exact Illinois "Work." Nearly 400 foot-notes from the highest Masonic authorities. Complete work of 640 pages, the First Seven Degrees comprising the Blue Lodge and the Chapter Degrees. Cloth $2.00

First 3 degrees, cloth... 1.25

REVISED FREEMASONRY ILLUSTRATED.

The complete and accurate ritual of the First Seven Masonic Degrees of the Blue Lodge and Chapter, by Jacob O. Doesburg, Past Master of Unity Lodge, Holland, Michigan, a Royal Arch Mason, with full Monitorial and Scripture readings and the Secret Work profusely illustrated. The exact Michigan "Work," with a Historical Sketch of the Order and a critical analysis of each degree by President J. Blanchard. Also the legal attestation of the accuracy of the ritual by the author and others.

Paper cover, $1.25; cloth, $2.00; First Three Degrees paper, 75c; cloth, $1.25.

STANDARD FREEMASONRY ILLUSTRATED.

The complete and accurate ritual of the First Seven Masonic Degrees of the Blue Lodge and Chapter, by a Past High Priest, with all Monitorial and Scripture Readings and the Secret Work fully illustrated. Nearly 400 foot-notes from the highest Masonic authorities. Complete work of 640 pages, the First Seven degrees comprising the Blue Lodge and the Chapter Degrees.

This book gives the "work" of the following twenty-six states:

Alabama, Arizona, Arkansas, Alaska, Colorado, Connecticut, Delaware, Florida, Georgia, Idaho, Indiana, Iowa, Oklahoma, Kentucky, Louisiana, Mississippi, Montana, Nebraska, New Mexico, Oregon, Rhode Island, South Carolina, Texas, Utah, Washington, Wyoming, Ontario, and Canada.

Cloth.....$2.00 , First 3 degrees, paper cover......75c; cloth.....$1.25.

THE MASTER'S CARPET;

By Edmond Ronayne, Past Master of Keystone Lodge, No. 639, Chicago. The work contains 406 pages, illustrated with 50 engravings, and is substantially bound in cloth.

Price, 90 cents.

Explains the true source and meaning of every ceremony and symbol of the Blue Lodge, showing the basis on which the ritual is founded. By a careful perusal of this work, a more thorough knowledge of the principles of the order can be obtained than by attending the Lodge for years. Every Mason, every person contemplating becoming a member, and even those who are indifferent on the subject, should procure and carefully read this work.

MAH-HAH-BONE;

By Edmond Ronayne. Bound in fine cloth. 690 pages, 135 illustrations. Price $2.00.

Comprises the "Hand Book of Free Masonry," "Master's Carpet," in one volume. The value and convenience of this combined book will be seen at once. As the Master's Carpet frequently refers by foot notes to the Hand Book, and the Hand Book as frequently refers to the "Carpet," by having both books under one cover, reference can be made in an instant. It is cheaper; as the Carpet at 90c and the Hand Book at $1.25 would make $2.15, while the combined book sells in fine cloth binding at $2.00.

CHAPTER DEGREES;

By Edmond Ronayne, Past Master of Keystone Lodge, No. 639, Chicago; Ex-Member of the Grand Lodge of Illinois, 312 pp. Paper, 75c, cloth,

Price $1.25.

This book gives the opening, closing, secret work and lectures of the Mark Master, Past Master, Most Excellent Master and Royal Arch Degrees, as set forth by the General Grand Royal Chapter of the United States of America. Completely illustrated with diagrams, figures and illustrations. It gives the correct method of conferring the degrees and the proper manner of conducting the business of the Lodge. The "secret work" is given in full, including the oaths, obligations, signs, grips and pass-words. All of which are correct and can be relied upon. The accuracy of this work has been attested by high and unimpeachable Masonic authority.

CHAPTER MASONRY ILLUSTRATED.

By Jacob O. Doesburg. The 4th to 7th degrees inclusive.

Cloth, $1.00

SCOTCH RITE MASONRY ILLUSTRATED.

The Complete Ritual of the Scottish Rite; 4th to 33rd Degrees inclusive, by a Sovereign Grand Commander. Profusely illustrated. The first Chapter is devoted to an Historical Sketch of the Rite, by President Blanchard, of Wheaton College, who also furnishes the Introduction and Analysis of the character of each degree. Over Four Hundred accurate quotations from the highest Masonic authorities (Three Hundred and Ninety-Nine of them footnotes) show the character and object of these degrees and also afford incontrovertible proof of the correctness of the Ritual. The work is issued in two volumes and comprises 1,038 pages. Per set (2 vols).

Cloth, $4.00; paper cover, $2.50

Explanatory.—Freemasonry illustrated and Knight Templarism illustrated give the 13 degrees of the York Rite, and there are 33 degrees in the Scottish Rite. But the first three degrees, as given in the first part of Free Masonry Illustrated, belong to both Rites. So these books give 43 different degrees (no duplicates).

KNIGHT TEMPLARISM ILLUSTRATED.

A full illustrated ritual of the six degrees of the Council and Commandery, comprising the degrees of Royal Master, Select Master, Super-Excellent Master, Knight of the Red Cross, Knight Templar and Knight of Malta. A book of 341 pages.

Paper covers, $1.25: Cloth, $2.00

THE MYSTIC SHRINE ILLUSTRATED.

Revised and enlarged edition. A complete illustrated Ritual of the Nobles of the Mystic Shrine. This is a side Masonic degree conferred only on Knights Templar and on Thirty-two degree Masons.

Paper cover, 40 cents; Cloth, 75 cents; Abridged Edition, Paper cover 25 cents each.

ADOPTIVE MASONRY ILLUSTRATED.

A full and complete ritual of the five Eastern Star or Ladies' Degrees, by Thomas Lowe, comprising the degrees of Jephthah's Daughter, Ruth, Esther, Martha and Electa, and known as the Daughter's Degree, Widow's Degree, Wife's Degree, Sister's Degree and the Benevolent Degree.

Paper cover, 50 cents; Cloth, 75 cents.

MASONIC OATHS;

By Edmond Ronayne, Past Master of Keystone Lodge, No. 639, Chicago, 183 pages. Paper cover, price 50 cents.

A masterly discussion of the Oaths of the Masonic Lodge, illustrating every sign, grip and ceremony of the Masonic Lodge. This work is highly commended by leading lecturers as furnishing the best arguments on the character of Masonic obligations of any book in print.

FREE MASONRY AT A GLANCE;

By Edmond Ronayne, Past Master Keystone Lodge, No. 639, Chicago, 32 pages. Price, postpaid, 15 cents. It illustrates every sign, grip and ceremony of the first three degrees, and gives a brief explanation of each.

FREEMASONRY EXPOSED.

By Captain William Morgan. The genuine old Morgan book republished with engravings showing the Lodge-room, dress of candidates, signs, due guards, grips, etc. Also portrait of the author and engraving of the monument erected to his memory at Batavia, N. Y., in 1882 by over two thousand contributors.

Paper cover, 25 cents; Cloth, 50 cents.

CONFESSION OF THE MURDER OF MORGAN.

In this Confession Henry L. Valance says that he was one of the three chosen by lot to drown Capt. Wm. Morgan in the Niagara River for exposing Free Masonry.

Paper cover, 10 cents each.

HISTORY OF THE ABDUCTION AND MURDER OF

"Capt Wm. Morgan." As prepared by seven committees of citizens, appointed to ascertain the fate of Morgan. This book contains indisputable legal evidence that Free Masons abducted and murdered Wm. Morgan, for no other offense than the revelation of Masonry.   **Price 35 cents**

THREE MASTER MASONS.

Library size, 400 pages, blue and gold; 126 questions answered, showing the lost or hidden language of the emblem. By Milton A. Pottenger, 32°. Endorsed by the highest Masonic authority.

Price, Post Paid, $2.50

"SYMBOLISM";

By Milton A. Pottenger, 32°. A book for Masons. A treatise on the soul of things. A pack of playing cards or book of fifty-two, an ancient Masonic Bible. The United States, a Masonic nation, whose birth, duty and destiny is prophesied and read in this book of ancient wisdom.

"Symbolism" throws a great light upon the hidden meaning and teachings of Masonic emblems. No officer or student of Masonry can afford to be without it. Every page full of wonders to the Mason. It is difficult for the American citizen to believe that there ever was a time when to be educated was to be a criminal. However, when one stops to realize that Monarchial forms of government are created, maintained and perpetuated by ignorance, superstition and intolerance, the Mason of high degree especially can see why education might become criminal.

The Standard Monitor.

Edward Cook (Not our publication). Leather, 50 cents.

Odd-Fellowship

REVISED ODD-FELLOWSHIP ILLUSTRATED.

The complete revised ritual of the Lodge, Encampment and Rebekah (ladies') degree. By a Past Grand Patriarch. Profusely illustrated and guaranteed to be strictly accurate, with the sketch of the origin, history and character of the order. Over one hundred foot note quotations from standard authorities, showing the character and teachings of the order and an analysis of each degree by President J. Blanchard. This book contains an exact copy of the late official "Charge Books" issued by the Sovereign Grand Lodge, with the secret work accurately given and profusely illustrated. In use all over America.

Paper covers, $1.00; Cloth, $1.50

REVISED REBEKAH RITUAL ILLUSTRATED.

Revised and Amended Official "Ritual for Rebekah Lodges, Published by the Sovereign Grand Lodge, I. O. O. F.," with the Unwritten (secret) work added and the official "Ceremonies of Instituting Rebekah Lodges and Installation of Officers of Rebekah Lodges."

Price paper covers, 45 cents; Cloth, 75 cents.

PATRIARCHS MILITANT ILLUSTRATED.

Adopted by the Sovereign Grand Lodge of the Independent Order of Odd-Fellows in September, 1885. An accurate copy of the Charge Book furnished by the Sovereign Grand Lodge, with the eighteen Military Diagrams and the Unwritten (Secret) Work added.

Paper cover, 85 cents each.